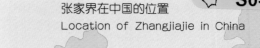

张家界在中国的位置
Location of Zhangjiajie in China

北京
Beijing

张家界　　长沙
Zhangjiajie ○　· Changsha

湖南
Hunan

目　录　Contents

Mountains

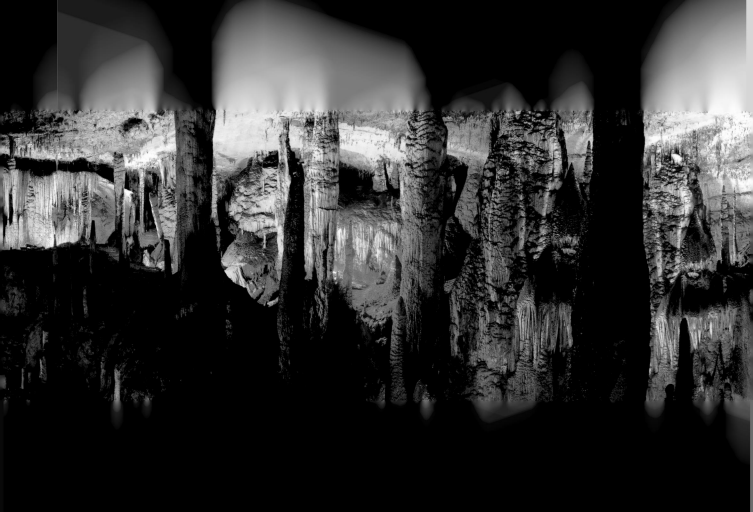

张家界市是1988年经国务院批准成立的省辖地级市，辖永定、武陵源两区和慈利、桑植两县，总人口150多万，总面积9563平方公里，市府设永定区，距省城长沙390公里，距长江三峡300公里。

张家界市具有丰富的世界一流的旅游资源，已列入自然风景区的五大片，约1000平方公里。最负盛名的是由张家界国家森林公园、索溪峪自然保护区、天子山自然保护区三大块组成的被联合国教科文组织列入《世界自然遗产名录》的武陵源风景名胜区。该景区总面积369平方公里，旅游景观以世界罕见的奇特的石英砂岩峰林为主，境内奇峰林立，怪石嶙峋，树茂林丰，溶洞群布，沟壑纵横，溪水潺潺，珍禽竞翅，奇花争妍，藏峰、桥、洞、湖于一体，汇名山大川之大成，被中外游客誉为"大自然的迷宫"、"中国山水画的原本"、"扩大了的盆景，缩小了的仙山"，不可思议的"天然博物馆"、"地球纪念物"。境内那些如柱、如鞭、如塔、似人、似禽、似兽的峰林石景，无不给人以美丽的遐想。覆盖率达90%以上的原始次森林既有大量古稀珍木、奇花异卉、名贵中草药，还有多种珍禽怪兽，如金钱豹、猕猴、灵猫、娃娃鱼、背水鸡、玻璃蛇、红嘴相思鸟等，构成一个天然的动植物王国；众多溶洞，景观丰富，造景绝妙，洞内钟乳遍布，石笋林立，洞中有洞，洞中有山、泉、瀑、河，幽深莫测，向人们展现出一个神话般的地下世界。《国际自然与自然资源保护联盟技术评价报告》中指出："武陵源在风景上可以和美国西部的几个国家森林公园及纪念物相比，武陵源具有不可否定的自然美。因为它拥有壮丽的参差不齐的石峰、郁郁葱葱的植被以及清澈的湖泊、溪流。"在武陵源外围，还有被联合国列入"人与生物圈"观测站的八大公山自然保护区，被誉为"武陵之魂"的天门山、"百里画廊"的茅岩河、"亚洲第一洞"的九天洞等风景区。此外，张家界市还是土家族、白族、苗族等少数民族聚居地，少数民族占总人口的72%，多姿多彩的民族风情与绝美的自然风景交相映衬，吸引了越来越多的中外游客。

经过十多年的努力，全市已开发旅游参观游览区(点)12个，建成游览线30多条，建成景区游道300多公里和景区登山索道两条。张家界火车站已与国内10多个大、中城市开通了旅客列车，张家界机场与国内20多个大、中城市开通了航班。张家界的邮电通讯已达国内先进水平，全市现有饭店400多家，床位总数已达3万多张，其中二星级以上饭店20余家，全市现有为旅游

In 1980's in the northwest of Hunan Province, a young city, which characterized by its tourism development, was founded.

Zhangjiajie is a province governed district city designated by the State Council in 1988. It administrates Yongding, Wulingyuan districts and Cili, Sangzhi counties, with its population of more than 1,500,000 and area 9563 square kilometers. The municipal government is located in Yongding District, which is 390 kilometers away from the capital Changsha and 300 kilometers from the Three Gorge in Yangtze River.

Zhangjiajie is abundant in world-leading tourist destinations. Five parts have already been selected as unspoiled scenic areas, covering about 1000 square kilometers. Among them, the most famous Wulingyuan scenic resort, which consists of Zhangjiajie National Forest Park, Suoxi Valley Reserve and Tianzi Mountain Reserve, was already listed into "the World Nature Heritage" by the UNESCO. It covers an area of 369 square kilometers with the quartz sandstone forest and peak as its major attraction. Inside the area, fantastic peaks stand in groups like the forest and jagged rocks take the grotesque shapes; luxuriant are the plants and forests; stalactite caverns are as many as the stars; Circles by valleys and gorges; it has limpid streams all over and boasts of the precious birds and singular flowers. Combining the peaks bridges, caves and lakes into one picturesque area, taking the advantages from the famous mountains and huge rivers, it is called "the labyrinth of nature", "the original of Chinese mountain and water painting", "the enlarged potted landscape and the decreased fairyland", "the inconceivable natural museum" and "the globe memorial". The stone forest, rocks and peaks, which resemble the pillars, whips, towers, human beings, animals and beasts, evoke tourists wild imagination and admiration. The land, 90% of which is covered by primitive forest, has not only old rare trees, singular blooms and precious herbs, but also rare animals and beasts, such as leopard, monkey, cat, giant salamander, water-carrying birds, glass snake, red-billed leiothrix and etc. In this plants and animals kingdom, the limestone caverns also provide the fabulous views by their excellent stalactites which can be seen everywhere. It is a world of stalactites. The bamboo-shoot shape rocks that stand side by side like jungle, together with the smaller caves, mountain springs, cascades and rivers in it, through the cooling darkness and unimaginable deepness, displays a mythical underground world.

As "The Evaluation Report of Protection Alliance for International Nature and Natural Resource" described, "Scenically speaking, Wulingyuan can compare favorably with the national forest parks of west America, for it has unresistable natural beauty, which comes from its spectacular peaks, luxuriant vegetation, limpid lakes and stream." Outside of Wulingyuan, there are still many other sightseeing areas: the Badagong Mount Reserve, which has been selected as the observation station of "Man And Biosphere" by the United Nations, the so called "Soul of Wuling"--Tianmen Mount., "50-KM gallery" --Maoyan River, "The Greatest cavern of Asia"--Jiutian Cavern and etc. Zhangjiajie is inhabited by Tujia, Bai, Miao and other ethnic groups. They account for 72 percent of the total population. Mixed with the varied culture and custom, the excellent natural scenery attracts more and more Chinese and foreign tourists.

In the wake of ten years' efforts, Zhangjiajie City has set up 12 excursion centers, which link 30 routs for sightseeing, cover a distance of over 300 kilometers and are equipped with two cable ways. Communications networks connect scenic spots and city proper as well as different scenic sites. Zhangjiajie Railway Station has access to more than 10 large and medium-sized cities through express trains, and airport is open to more than 20 large and medium-sized cities. The city's telecommunications system has reached advanced level at home. The city boasts more than 400 hotels, which afford accommodation for over 30,000 tourists. Over 20 of the hotels are graded as star level. Besides, it possesses over 50 travel agencies.

As it is becoming better known to the world and its tourist facilities improving and its ports opened, Zhangjiajie is quickening its steps to go the world arena.

Welcome friends from home and abroad to Zhangjiajie!

张家界国家森林公园
Zhangjiajie National Forest Park

　　张家界森林公园是我国第一个国家森林公园。

　　该公园属石英砂岩峰林地貌，景自天成。峰奇、谷幽、石怪、水秀。"原始风光自然美"是其最大特色。这里植被丰茂，森林覆盖率达97%以上，成片原始次森林里，珍禽怪兽出没其间，奇花异草四季飘香，稀世珍木数不胜数。

Zhangjiajie is the first national forest park in China.

The landscape of the park is quartz rock forest. It is a nature created fairy-land with fabulous peaks deep valleys, peculiar rocks and limpid water. Charaterized by its primitive and natural beauty, it is full of luxuriant vegetation. 97% of its land is coated with forests. The vastly stretched primitive forests is the haunt of rare animals and beasts. Singular blooms and peculiar herbs breathe their fragrances in all season. Countless are the unusual trees.

五指峰
Five-finger Peaks

蓬莱仙境　Fairyland

六奇阁 Pavilion of Six Wonders

雾锁奇峰　Rare Peak in Fogs

后花园
Back Garden

天下第一桥　The Highest Natural Bridge on Earth

迷魂台　Mihun Terrace

金鞭溪
Jinbian Stream

　　金鞭溪因其上游一著名景观金鞭岩而得名。全长6公里，自西向东蜿蜒于奇峰峡谷间，水随山转、山因水活、一步一景，如画如诗。

　　Jinbian Stream gets the name from the famous Jinbian Rock which lies in its headwaters. Meandering from west to east among the fantastic peaks and valleys, it takes the length of 8 kilometers. Water vivifies the mountains and mountain directs the water. The views differ from each step and make Jinbian Stream a dreamland of picture and poem.

金鞭岩　Golden Whip Rock

千里相会　Meeting after Long Journey

　彩泉　Colorful Spring

翠涧　Meandering Stream Through Green Valley

幽谷翠影 Beautiful Reflection in the Valley   倾听 Listening

水绕四门　Water Flowing four Ways

天子山自然保护区
Tianzi Mount. Reserve

天子山因古代土家族首领向王天子在此起义而得名。

天子山为台地地貌，地势高，四面皆可观景，环山游览线有45公里，景区总面积67平方公里。在天子山观景，视野开阔，层次丰富，峰中有峰，峰外有峰。"云雾、月夜、霞日、冬雪"堪称天子山四大奇观。

Tianzi Mount. is named after the Tujia people(Native people) rebellion chief Xiangwang Tianzi(Emperor xiangwang). The platform, rising above the surrounding countryside, is the most conspicuous feature of Tianzi Mountain. The sightseeing line circles the mountain 45 kilometers.The total area covers 67 square kilometers.Looking from Tianzi Mountain, you will get the broad sight of peaks in peaks, peaks beyond peaks. "Cloudy mist, moon night, sun rising from the morning clouds and the snow" are the four spectaculars of Tianzi Mount..

云山陶醉图　Beautiful Clouds and Peak

晖映御笔　Imperoial Pen Peak

银装素裹 Winter of Tianzi Mountain

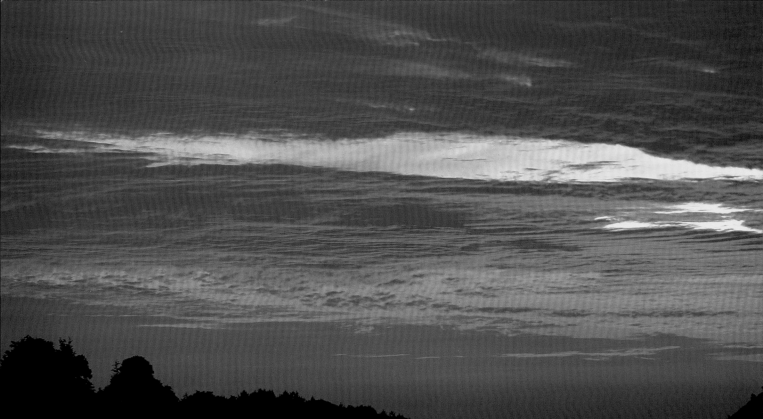

神堂湾
Shengtang Gulf

云青岩　Beautiful Peaks at Yunqing Crag

鸳鸯瀑布　Quail Falls

大观台　Grand Sightseeing Terrace

空中田园　Fields in the sky　　　　　神兵聚会 Heavenly Warriors' Gathering

索溪峪自然保护区

索溪峪"因溪水状如绳索而得名"。

该景区属多层石英砂岩峰林地貌，因在地质发育后期，不仅在地上造就了奇特的石英砂岩峰林，而且在地下也营造了神秘的溶洞群。境内奇峰错落，溪壑纵横，怪石嶙峋，洞天迷离，山景、水景、洞景浑然一体。

Suoxi Valley Reserve

Suoxi Valley Reserve is so "named because of its rope-like stream course."

The landscape of this area is the quartz stone forest and peaks. Formed at the end of geological developing period , its reaction was much stronger than Zhangjiajie Park, thus it created not only the quartz stone forests and peaks on the ground,but also groups of stalactite caves underground. In this area, the unusual peaks and rocks , with streams and gorges circling among them, mixed with the caves and sky, make it a peerless scenery.

春的武陵源 Spring of Wuling yuan

铜墙铁壁　Sunshine on Peaks

秋染卧龙岭　Autumn of Wolongling

天台观秋　Mountain woods Dyed Crimson by Autumn leaves

西海峰林　Spectacle of Peaks

南天门　South Heaven Gate

宝峰湖

　　宝峰湖是武陵源风景区中的精品景点。它是一座罕见的高峡平湖，四面青山，一泓碧水，湖光山色，风光旖旎，是山水风景杰作，是人间瑶池。在此荡舟，还可见到湖心岛上"玉瓶开花"、"十女梳妆"、"金龟戏水"、"青蛙闹春"等佳景。

Baofeng Lake

　　Baofeng Lake is a rare high gorges lake and regarded as the elite scenic spot. The limpid lake, embraced by the green mountains, mirrors its hilloettes and makes it a scenic masterpiece. Boating here, you can see Jade Bottle with Flowers Blossoming, Ten Girls Combing Hair, Gold Turtle Playing with Water, Frogs Singing for the Spring and other scenic spots in the central island of the lake.

宝峰飞瀑　Baofeng Falls

深山藏古寺　An Old Temple in the Mountain

黄龙洞

　　黄龙洞是武陵源风景区的王牌景点。黄龙洞分四层，高达160余米，深15公里，面积约20公顷。洞内有1库、2河、3瀑、4潭、13厅、46廊，洞内钟乳石繁多而珍奇，石笋、石柱、石幔、石瀑、石川、石鞭、石花等晶莹剔透，琳琅满目。黄龙洞是世界上已经发现的溶洞的"全能冠军"。

Huanglong Cavern

Huanglong Cavern is the peerless scenic spot among Wulingyuan. Divided into 4 levels from the top to the bottom, Huanglong Cavern has vertical height up to 160 meters and 15 kilometers long. The discovered sightseeing area is about 20 hectares. Now it is known there are 13 halls, 46 corridor, 3 waterfalls and 1 underground river. Areas in the cavern consist of "dragon palace", "rattle river", "fairy water", "paradise pillar street". It is abundant in fantastic stalactites. Taking the shape of bamboo shoot, pillar, curtain, waterfall, river, whip and flower, the stones display a wonderful world with its transparent and glittering looking. Huanglong Cavern almost covers the whole knowledge of caverns, for it is the "all-round champion" over all the other caverns found in the world at present.

定海神针　Magic Needle

迷宫　Beautiful Stalactites

京迷工宇 Column Shaped Stalactites

九天洞

　　九天洞，因有九个天窗而得名，人称"亚洲第一洞"，总面积达 260 万平方米。

　　大、奇、美、幽，是九天洞的四大特色。洞内有 40 厅、3 河、5 桥、6 山、7 湖、8 处千丘田、10 瀑及不可胜数的钟乳石群。

Jiutian Cavern

Named after its 9 windows facing the sky, Jiutian Cavern is regarded as "Greatest Cavern In Asia", for it has 2.6 million square meters.

This expanse,unique,picturesque and tranquil cavern is separated into 3 stories which are connected by 5 spiral viewing places in different height. For the time being, we know in this cavern, there are 40 halls, 3 underground rivers, 5 natural bridges, 6 inner mountains, 7 small lakes, 8 stair fields, 10 waterfalls and numerous stalactite.

天门山

　　天门山别称云梦山、玉屏山，因三国吴永安六年发生地震，天门洞开，始得其名，海拔1517.9米。天门山自然景观奇特，有16峰16洞，尤以天门洞叫绝。人文景观则首推天门山寺，香火千百年来长明不熄，闻名于江南各省。

Tianmen Mount.

　　In ancient time, Tianmen Mount was called: Yunmen Mount., Yuping Mount., but in 6th of Yongan in Three-Kingdom Dynasty, there happened an earthquake, then a giant gap opened, therefore it got this name since then. With the altitude of 1517.9M, Tianmen Mount. has pretty unique natural prospects. Among its 16 peaks & 16 caverns, the Tianmen Cavern is the most special one. For the cultural prospects, Tianmen Mount. Temple is recommended. With its reputation throughout the provinces bf Southern Yangtze River, it makes the visitors coming and oil lights shining for centuries.

天门山之晨　Morning Sunshine over Tianmen Mountain

画中游　Drifting on the Maoyan River

茅岩河漂流

与浪共舞——茅岩河漂流

Drifting on the Maoyan River

Dancing with Waves—Drifting on the Maoyan River

梯玛　Sacrificial Ceremony

　揭头盖　Amorous Wedding Night

供奉祭品　Sacrificial Offerings

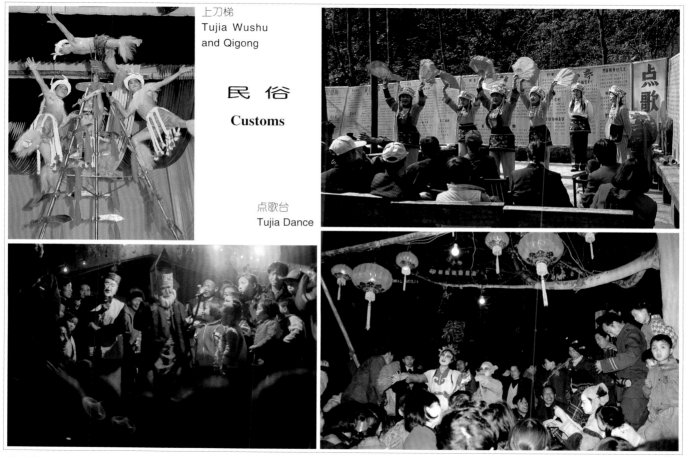

上刀梯
Tujia Wushu
and Qigong

民 俗
Customs

点歌台
Tujia Dance

土地戏　Village God Performance

花灯戏　Festival lantern Display

东海云涛　Swirling Clouds on East sea Mountain

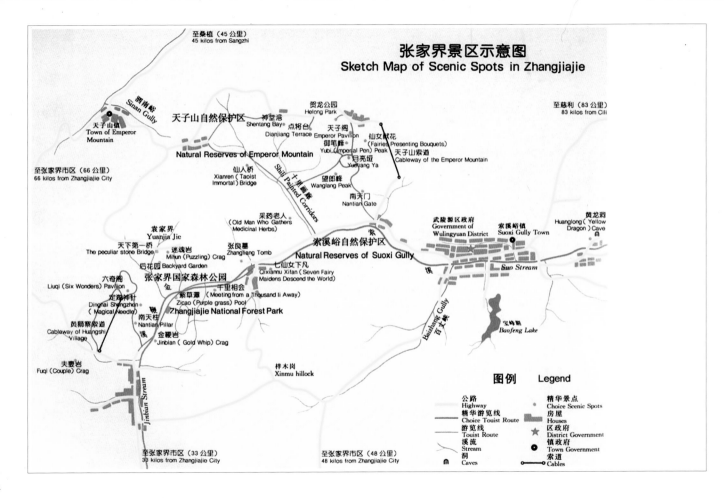

张家界景区示意图
Sketch Map of Scenic Spots in Zhangjiajie

至桑植（45公里）
45 kilos from Sangzhi

至慈利（83公里）
83 kilos from Cili

泗南峪
Sinan Gully

天子山镇
Town of Emperor
Mountain

天子山自然保护区
Natural Reserves of Emperor Mountain

贺龙公园
Helong Park

神堂湾
Shentang Bay

点将台
Dianjiang Terrace

天子阁
Emperor Pavilion

御笔峰
Yubi (Imperial Pen) Peak

仙女献花
(Fairies Presenting Bouquets)

天子山索道
Cableway of the Emperor Mountain

月亮垭
Yueyang Ya

至张家界市区（66公里）
66 kilos from Zhangjiajie City

仙人桥
Xianren (Taoist
Immortal) Bridge

望郎峰
Wanglang Peak

南天门
Nantian Gate

十里画廊
Shili Painted Corridors

采药老人
(Old Man Who Gathers
Medicinal Herbs)

武陵源区政府
Government of
Wulingyuan District

索溪峪镇
Suoxi Gully Town

黄龙洞
Huanglong (Yellow
Dragon) Cave

袁家界
Yuanjia Jie

天下第一桥
The peculiar stone Bridge

迷魂岩
Mihun (Puzzling) Crag

张良墓
Zhangliang Tomb

索溪峪自然保护区
Natural Reserves of Suoxi Gully

后花园
Backyard Garden

张家界国家森林公园
Zhangjiajie National Forest Park

七仙女下凡
Qixiannu Xifan (Seven Fairy
Maidens Descend the World)

索溪
Suo Stream

六奇阁
Liuqi (Six Wonders) Pavilion

定海神针
Dinghai Shengzhen
(Magical Needle)

千里相会
(Meeting from a Thousand li Away)

紫草潭
Zicao (Purple grass) Pool

黄狮寨索道
Cableway of Huangshi
Village

南天柱
Nantian Pillar

金鞭岩
Jinbian (Gold Whip) Crag

百丈峡
Baizhang Gully

宝峰湖
Baofeng Lake

夫妻岩
Fuqi (Couple) Crag

金鞭溪
Jinbian Stream

梓木岗
Xinmu hillock

至张家界市区（33公里）
33 kilos from Zhangjiajie City

至张家界市区（48公里）
48 kilos from Zhangjiajie City

图例　　Legend

公路
Highway

精华游览线
Choice Touist Route

游览线
Touist Route

溪流
Stream

洞
Caves

精华景点
Choice Scenic Spots

房屋
Houses

区政府
District Government

镇政府
Town Government

索道
Cables